What's The Best Little Illustrated Riddle Book?

200 Riddles and Brain Teasers for All Ages

David Fickes

Introduction

Besides their entertainment value, riddles and brain teasers have important brain fitness benefits for all ages. They help prevent cognitive decline, improve problem-solving skills, enhance creativity, improve concentration, enhance spatial and visual reasoning, and even boost IQ. They can also reduce stress, promote relaxation, and enhance mood.

This book has 200 riddles and brain teasers, including periodic illustrations, to entertain and amuse all ages; for quick and easy feedback, it is formatted with a page of questions followed by a page of answers. It is designed to be compact, so you can read and enjoy it whenever and wherever you like.

If you enjoyed this book and would like others to enjoy it also, please put out a review or rating.

Questions 1

1) I left my campsite and hiked south for 3 miles; then, I turned east and hiked for 3 miles. Finally, I turned north and hiked for 3 miles and came upon a bear inside my tent eating my food. What color was the bear?

2) Three doctors said that John was their brother; John says he has no brothers. How many brothers does John have?

3) What does man love more than life and hate more than death; contented men desire; the poor have; the rich require; the miser spends; the spendthrift saves, and all men carry to their graves?

4) Four people arrive at a river with a bridge that can only hold two people at a time. It's night, and they only have one flashlight that must be used when crossing. Person A can cross the bridge in one minute, B in two minutes, C in five minutes, and D in eight minutes. When two people cross the bridge together, they must move at the slower person's pace. Can they all get across the bridge in 15 minutes or less?

5) What do an island and the letter "t" have in common?

Answers 1

1) White – The only place you can hike 3 miles south, 3 miles east, and 3 miles north, and end up back at your starting point is the North Pole, so it had to be a polar bear.

2) None – He has three sisters.

3) Nothing

4) First, A and B cross the bridge, and A brings the light back. This takes 3 minutes. Next, C and D cross, and B brings the light back. This takes another 10 minutes. Finally, A and B cross again, which takes another 2 minutes for a total of 15 minutes.

5) They are both in the middle of water.

Questions 2

6) What always runs but never walks, often murmurs, never talks, has a bed but never sleeps, has a mouth but never eats?

7) A man wanted to enter an exclusive club but did not know the password. He waited by the door and listened. A member knocked on the door, and the doorman said, "twelve." The member replied, "six" and was let in. A second member came to the door, and the doorman said, "six." The member replied, "three" and was let in. The man thought he had heard enough and walked up to the door. The doorman said, "ten," and the man replied, "five," but he was not let in. What should he have said?

8) The person who makes it has no need for it. The person who buys it has no use for it. The person who uses it can neither see nor feel it. What is it?

9) What is always in front of you but can't be seen?

10) What comes once in a minute, twice in a moment, but never in a thousand years?

Answers 2

6) A river

7) Three – The password is based on the number of letters in the word he says.

8) Coffin

9) Future

10) Letter m

Questions 3

11) At night, they come without being fetched. By day, they are lost without being stolen. What are they?

12) If 5 elves take 5 minutes to make 5 toys, then how long will it take 100 elves to make 100 toys?

13) The more of this there is, the less you see. What is it?

14) A man who was outside in the rain without an umbrella or hat didn't get a single hair on his head wet. Why?

15) Forward it's heavy; backward it's not. What is it?

Answers 3

11) The stars

12) 5 minutes – One elf can make a toy in 5 minutes, so 100 elves can make 100 toys in 5 minutes.

13) Darkness

14) He was bald.

15) Ton

Questions 4

16) A man is condemned to death and must choose between three rooms. The first room is full of raging fires; the second has assassins with loaded guns, and the third has lions who haven't eaten in years. Which room is the safest?

17) What month of the year has 28 days?

18) I am a word of letters three; add two, and fewer there will be. What word am I?

19) I have a large money box, 10 inches wide and 5 inches tall. About how many coins can I place in it until my money box is no longer empty?

20) What four-letter word, typed in all capital letters, can be written forward, backward, or upside down, and can still be read from left to right?

Answers 4

16) The room with the lions because they would have starved to death.

17) All of them

18) Few

19) One – After that, it won't be empty.

20) NOON

Questions 5

21) Where is there no south, west, nor east, and weather not fit for man or beast?

22) What breaks yet never falls, and what falls yet never breaks?

23) What can you keep after giving to someone?

24) I make two people out of one. What am I?

25) I can be cracked; I can be made. I can be told; I can be played. What am I?

Answers 5

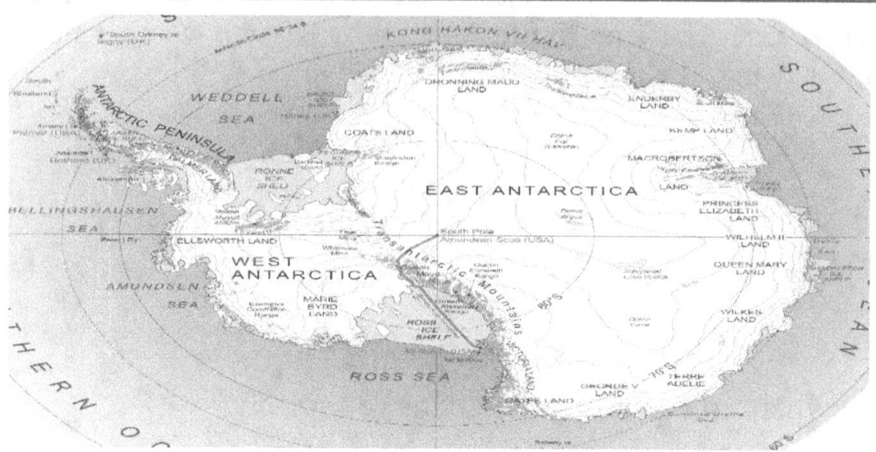

21) South Pole

22) Day and night

23) Your word

24) Mirror

25) Joke

Questions 6

26) You throw away the outside and cook the inside. Then you eat the outside and throw away the inside. What did you eat?

27) A man stands on one side of a river; his dog is on the other side. The man calls his dog, who immediately crosses the river without getting wet and without using a bridge or a boat. How did the dog do it?

28) What English word does the following: the first two letters signify a male; the first three letters signify a female; the first four letters signify a great person, while the entire word signifies a great woman. What is the word?

29) What 5-letter word typed in all capital letters can be read the same upside down?

30) What belongs to you, but other people use it more than you?

Answers 6

26) An ear of corn

27) The river was frozen.

28) Heroine

29) SWIMS

30) Your name

Questions 7

31) I have two arms, but fingers none. I have two feet but cannot run. While I carry well, I have found I carry best with my feet off the ground. What am I?

32) I speak without a mouth and hear without ears. I have no body, but I come alive with the wind. What am I?

33) I follow you all the time and copy your every move, but you can't touch me or catch me. What am I?

34) A king, queen, and two twins all lay in a large room. How are there no adults in the room?

35) I am going out when you are sad or when you are happy. Other times you want to hide me, but it's hard, so please don't try it. What am I?

Answers 7

31) Wheelbarrow

32) Echo

33) Your shadow

34) They are all beds.

35) Tears

Questions 8

36) What continues to go up and down without moving?

37) The number 8,549,176,320 is a unique number. What is so special about it?

38) A merchant can place 8 large boxes or 10 small boxes into a carton for shipping. In one shipment, he sent a total of 96 boxes. If there are more large boxes than small boxes, how many cartons did he ship?

39) What is bought by the yard but is worn by the foot?

40) You walk into a creepy house by yourself. There is no electricity, plumbing, or ventilation. You notice 3 doors with numbers on them. Once you open the doors you will die a particular way. Through the first door, you'll be eaten by a hungry lion. Through the second door, you'll be stabbed to death. Through the third door, you will be killed in an electric chair. Which door do you pick?

Answers 8

36) Stairs

37) It has the numbers 0-9 in alphabetical order.

38) 11 cartons total

39) Carpet

40) The third door since there is no electricity to harm you.

Questions 9

41) A pet shop owner had a parrot with a sign on its cage that said, "Parrot repeats everything it hears." Mike bought the parrot and spoke to it for two weeks, and it didn't say a word. He returned the parrot, but the shopkeeper said he never lied about the parrot. How can this be true?

42) When John was six years old, he hammered a nail into his favorite tree to mark his height. Ten years later at age sixteen, John returned to see how much higher the nail was. If the tree grew by two inches each year, how much higher would the nail be?

43) There's a one-story house where everything is yellow – yellow walls, yellow doors, yellow furniture. What color are the stairs?

44) You see me once in June, twice in November, and not at all in May. What am I?

45) Can you write down eight eights, so they add up to 1,000?

Answers 9

41) The parrot was deaf.

42) The nail would be at the same height since trees grow at their tops.

43) There aren't any because it's a one-story house.

44) The letter e

45) 888 + 88 + 8 + 8 + 8 = 1000.

Questions 10

46) A man is walking down a road with a basket of eggs. As he is walking, he meets someone who buys one-half of his eggs plus one-half of an egg. He walks a little further and meets another person who buys one-half of his eggs plus one-half of an egg. After going further, he meets another person who buys one-half of his eggs plus one-half of an egg. At this point, he has sold all his eggs, and he never broke an egg. How many eggs did the man have to start with?

47) You see a boat filled with people, yet there isn't a single person on board. How is that possible?

48) A doctor and a bus driver are both in love with the same woman, an attractive girl named Linda. The bus driver had to go on a long bus trip that would last a week. Before he left, he gave Linda seven apples. Why?

49) What do you bury when it is alive and dig up when it is dead?

50) What kind of cheese is made backward?

Answers 10

46) 7 eggs. The first person bought one-half of his eggs plus one-half of an egg (3 1/2 + 1/2 = 4 eggs), leaving 3 eggs. The second person bought one-half of his eggs plus one-half of an egg (1 1/2 + 1/2 = 2 eggs), leaving 1 egg. The last person bought one-half of his eggs plus one-half of an egg, (1/2 + 1/2 = 1 egg), leaving no eggs.

47) All the people are married.

48) An apple a day keeps the doctor away.

49) Plant

50) Edam

Questions 11

51) A duck was given $9; a spider was given $36, and a bee was given $27. Based on this information, how much money would a cat get?

52) I am something people love or hate. I change people's appearances and thoughts. If a person takes care of themselves, I will go up even higher. To some people, I will fool them. To others, I am a mystery. Some people might want to try and hide me, but I will show. No matter how hard people try, I will never go down. What am I?

53) A woman shoots her husband. Then she holds him underwater for over 5 minutes. Finally, she hangs him. But 5 minutes later, they both go out together and enjoy dinner together. How can this be?

54) An Arab sheik must leave his fortune to one of his two sons. He proposes that both sons ride their camels in a race, and whichever camel crosses the finish line last will win the fortune for its owner. During the race, the two brothers wander aimlessly for days, neither willing to cross the finish line. In desperation, they ask a wise man for advice. He tells them something, and the brothers leap onto the camels and charge toward the finish line. What did the wise man say?

55) A man looks at a painting in a museum and says, "Brothers and sisters I have none, but that man's father is my father's son." Who is in the painting?

Answers 11

51) $18 – $4.50 per leg

52) Age

53) The woman was a photographer. She shot a picture of her husband, developed it, and hung it up to dry.

54) The rules of the race were that the owner of the camel that crosses the finish line last wins the fortune. The wise man told them to switch camels.

55) The man's son

Questions 12

56) Five apples are in a basket. How do you divide them among five girls so that each girl gets an apple, but one apple remains in the basket?

57) An elevator is on the ground floor. There are five people in the elevator, including me. When the elevator reaches the first floor, one person gets out, and two people get in. The elevator goes up to the second floor, and five people get in. It then goes up to the next floor, no one gets out, but twelve people get in. Halfway up to the next floor, the elevator cable snaps, and it crashes to the ground. Everyone else dies in the elevator except me. How did I survive?

58) If you've got me, you want to share me; if you share me, you haven't kept me. What am I?

59) How do you make the number 7 even without addition, subtraction, multiplication, or division?

60) As I was going to St. Ives, I met a man with seven wives; each wife had seven sacks; each sack had seven cats; each cat had seven kits. Kits, cats, sacks, and wives, how many were going to St. Ives?

Answers 12

56) Give the fifth girl her apple in the basket.

57) I got off on the first floor.

58) A secret

59) Drop the s

60) One

Questions 13

61) What has six faces, but does not wear makeup; has twenty-one eyes, but cannot see?

62) What question can you never answer yes to?

63) A man was found dead next to a 13-story building. The police say it was a suicide, but you say it was a homicide. To prove this, you go to each floor of the building and open the window and toss a penny out. You do this to each floor until you reach the 13th floor and open the window and toss a penny out. How does this prove it wasn't a suicide?

64) Two girls have the same parents and were born at the same hour on the same day of the same month, but they are not twins. How can this be possible?

65) A girl has as many brothers as sisters, but each brother has only half as many brothers as sisters. How many brothers and sisters are there in the family?

Answers 13

61) A die (dice)

62) Are you asleep?

63) If the man committed suicide, he would have left the window open, and you wouldn't have had to open it.

64) They were not born in the same year.

65) Four sisters and three brothers

Questions 14

66) My life can be measured in hours; I serve by being devoured. Thin, I am quick. Fat, I am slow. The wind is my foe. What am I?

67) Rearrange the letters, O O U S W T D N E J R, to spell just one word. What is it?

68) What three numbers, none of which is zero, give the same result whether they're all added together or multiplied together?

69) What English word retains the same pronunciation, even after you take away four of its five letters?

70) Joe has ten coins totaling $1.19. From these coins, he can't make exact change for a dollar, half dollar, quarter, dime, or a nickel. What are the coins?

Answers 14

66) Candle

67) "Just one word"

68) 1, 2, 3

69) Queue

70) A half dollar, a quarter, four dimes, and four pennies

Questions 15

71) What has a head, a tail, is brown, and has no legs?

72) There are three playing cards in a row. Can you name them with these clues? There is a two to the right of a king. A diamond is left of a spade. An ace is to the left of a heart. A heart is to the left of a spade. Identify all three cards.

73) A farmer needs to take a fox, a chicken, and a sack of grain across a river. The only way across the river is by a small boat, which can only hold the farmer and one of the three items. Left unsupervised, the chicken will eat the grain, and the fox will eat the chicken. However, the fox won't try to eat the grain, and neither the fox nor the chicken will wander off. How does the farmer get everything across the river?

74) Often held but never touched; always wet but never rusts; often bites but seldom bit. To use me well, you must have wit. What am I?

75) A boy was at a carnival and went to a booth where a man said to the boy, "If I write your exact weight on this piece of paper then you have to give me $50, but if I cannot, I will pay you $50." The boy looked around and saw no scale, so he agrees, thinking no matter what the man writes he'll just say he weighs more or less. In the end, the boy ended up paying the man $50. How did the man win the bet?

Answers 15

71) Penny

72) Ace of diamonds, king of hearts, two of spades

73) Take the chicken across the river; come back with an empty boat. Take the grain across the river; bring the chicken back. Take the fox across the river; come back with an empty boat. Take the chicken across the river.

74) Tongue

75) The man did exactly as he said he would and wrote "your exact weight" on the paper.

Questions 16

76) I am not alive, but I grow; I don't have lungs, but I need air; I don't have a mouth, but water kills me. What am I?

77) Four cars come to a four-way stop, all coming from different directions. They can't decide who got there first, so they all go forward at the same time. They do not crash into each other, but all four cars go. How is this possible?

78) Mary has four daughters, and each of her daughters has a brother. How many children does Mary have?

79) Two in a corner, one in a room, zero in a house, but one in a shelter. What is it?

80) Alex's dad has 3 daughters, Marie, Christine, and what's the name of the third daughter?

Answers 16

76) Fire

77) They all made right-hand turns.

78) Five – Each daughter has the same brother.

79) The letter r

80) Alex

Questions 17

81) What can be driven although it doesn't have wheels, sliced but stays whole?

82) The water level in a reservoir is low, but it doubles every day. It takes 60 days to fill the reservoir. How long does it take for the reservoir to be half full?

83) Without the first two letters, I'm an intelligent animal. Without the first three letters, I'm a subject in school, and without the first four letters, I'm the letter "e." What am I?

84) There is a common English word that is nine letters long. Each time you remove a letter, it remains an English word, from nine letters down to a single letter. What is the original word, and what are the words that it becomes after removing one letter at a time?

85) There are 20 people in an empty, square room. Each person has full sight of the entire room and everyone in it without turning their head or body or moving in any way, other than their eyes. Where can you place an apple so that all but one person can see it?

Answers 17

81) Golf ball

82) 59 days – If the water level doubles every day, it was half full on day 59, not on day 30.

83) Grape

84) The base word is startling – starting, staring, string, sting, sing, sin, in, I.

85) Place the apple on one person's head.

Questions 18

86) When does Christmas come before Thanksgiving?

87) What is unusual about the following words: revive, banana, grammar, voodoo, assess, potato, dresser, uneven?

88) What is so fragile that saying its name breaks it?

89) Always in you, sometimes on you. If I surround you, I can kill you. What am I?

90) Find a number less than 100 that is increased by one-fifth of its value when its digits are reversed.

Answers 18

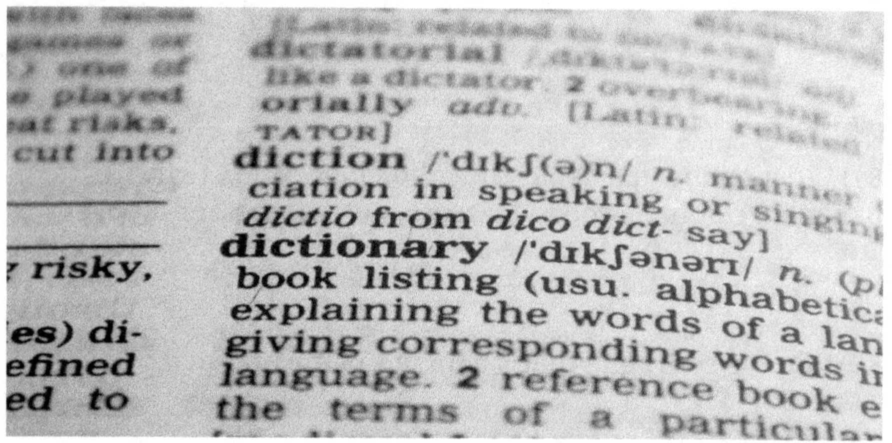

86) In the dictionary

87) Take the first letter of each word and place it at the end. It will spell the same word backward.

88) Silence

89) Water

90) 45 – (1/5 of 45 = 9, 9 + 45 = 54).

Questions 19

91) You walk into a room that contains a match, a kerosene lamp, a candle, and a fireplace. What would you light first?

92) A group of privates was standing facing due west. Their sergeant shouts at them: Right face! About face! Left face! In which direction are they now facing?

93) A man describes his daughters saying, "They are all blonde but two, all brunette but two, and all redhead but two." How many daughters does he have?

94) Jeff is younger than Mike but older than Karen. Larry is older than Erica, who is older than Jeff. Mike is older than Larry. Who is the middle child?

95) I have two coins equaling fifteen cents. One of them is not a nickel. What are the two coins?

Answers 19

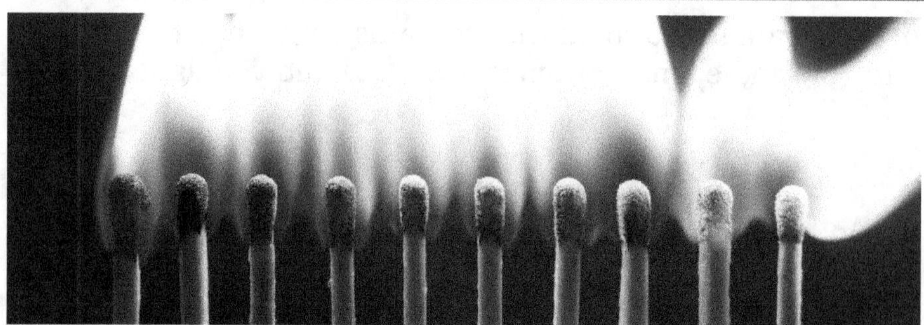

91) The match

92) East

93) Three - a blonde, a brunette, and a redhead

94) Erica

95) A dime and a nickel - One of the coins is not a nickel, but the other one is.

Questions 20

96) What gets wet while drying?

97) Once you are given one, you either have two or none?

98) The Barber of Seville shaves all men living in Seville; no man living in Seville is allowed to shave himself. The barber of Seville lives in Seville. Who shaves the barber of Seville?

99) Bob and David were preparing to have a water balloon fight. Bob says, "You have 3 times as many as I do," so David gives Bob 10 more balloons. Bob says, "You still have twice as many as I do." How many more balloons must David give Bob for them to have the same number?

100) A man dies of old age on his 25th birthday. How is this possible?

Answers 20

96) Towel

97) Choice

98) Nobody – The Barber of Seville is a woman.

99) David must give Bob another 20 water balloons, giving them each 60. Bob started with 30 water balloons and David with 90.

100) He was born on February 29.

Questions 21

101) My life is often a volume of grief; your help is needed to turn a new leaf. Stiff is my spine, and my body is pale, but I'm always ready to tell a tale. What am I?

102) Why can you not trust atoms?

103) While going toward the river, a rabbit saw nine elephants. Each elephant saw three monkeys going toward the river. Each monkey had one parrot in each hand. How many animals are going toward the river?

104) Fourteen of the children in the class are girls. Eight of the children wear blue shirts. Two of the children are neither girls nor wear a blue shirt. If five of the children are girls who wear blue shirts, how many children are in the class?

105) Everyone needs it, and everyone gives it, but no one takes it when you give it to them. What am I?

Answers 21

101) Book

102) Because they make up everything.

103) Ten animals are going towards the river – one rabbit, three monkeys, six parrots.

104) 19

105) Advice

Questions 22

106) The more you take, the more you leave behind. What are they?

107) A bus driver was heading down a street. He went right past a stop sign without stopping; he turned left where there was a no left turn sign, and he went the wrong way on a one-way street. Then he went on the left side of the road past a police car. Yet, he didn't break any traffic laws. Why not?

108) Two men were playing tennis. They played five sets, and each man won three sets. How can this be possible?

109) I am the beginning of the end and the end of time and space. I am essential to creation, and I surround every place. What am I?

110) What gets bigger when more is taken away?

Answers 22

106) Footsteps

107) He was walking, not driving.

108) The two men were partners playing doubles.

109) Letter e – End, timE, spacE, Every placE

110) Hole

Questions 23

111) What is black when it's clean and white when it's dirty?

112) If you have a 7-minute hourglass and an 11-minute hourglass, how can you boil an egg in exactly 15 minutes?

113) Can you name three consecutive days without using the words Monday, Tuesday, Wednesday, Thursday, Friday, Saturday, or Sunday?

114) A is the brother of B. B is the brother of C. C is the father of D. So how is D related to A?

115) If you're running in a race and you pass the person in second place, what place are you in?

Answers 23

111) Chalkboard

112) Start both hourglasses as you start boiling the egg. After the 7-minute hourglass runs out, turn it over to start it again. Four minutes later, when the 11-minute hourglass runs out, turn the 7-minute hourglass again. Wait for the 7-minute hourglass to run out, which will take another four minutes and get you to exactly 15 minutes of boiling time.

113) Yesterday, today, and tomorrow.

114) A is D's aunt

115) Second place

Questions 24

116) What is black when you buy it, red when you use it, and gray when you throw it away?

117) You are in a room that has three switches and a closed door. The switches control three light bulbs on the other side of the door. Once you open the door, you may never touch the switches again. How can you definitively tell which switch is connected to each of the light bulbs?

118) Two fathers and two sons are in a car, yet there are only three people in the car. How?

119) What five-letter word becomes shorter when you add two letters to it?

120) What is the only number spelled out in English that has its letters in alphabetical order?

Answers 24

116) Charcoal

117) Turn on the first two switches; leave them on for several minutes. Once five minutes have passed, turn off the second switch, leaving one switch on and go through the door. The light that is still on is connected to the first switch. Whichever of the other two bulbs is warm to the touch is connected to the second switch. The cold bulb is connected to the switch that was never turned on.

118) Grandfather, father, and son

119) Short

120) Forty

Questions 25

121) A man rode out of town on Sunday; he stayed a whole night at a hotel and rode back to town the next day on Sunday. How is this possible?

122) What word in the dictionary is spelled incorrectly?

123) I am a seven-letter word. I am very heavy. Take away two letters from me and you will get 8. Take away one letter and you will get 80. Who am I?

124) Spelled forward, I'm what you do every day, spelled backward, I'm something you hate. What am I?

125) Turn me on my side, and I am everything. Cut me in half, and I am nothing. What am I?

Answers 25

121) His horse was called Sunday.

122) Incorrectly

123) Weighty

124) Live

125) The number 8

Questions 26

126) My voice is tender; my waist is slender, and I'm often invited to play. Yet wherever I go I must take my bow or else I have nothing to say. What am I?

127) Until I am measured, I am not known. Yet how you miss me when I have flown. What am I?

128) Spelled out in English, what is the first number alphabetically?

129) What kind of coat is always wet when you put it on?

130) I can be written down; I can be spoken; I can be revealed; I can be broken. What am I?

Answers 26

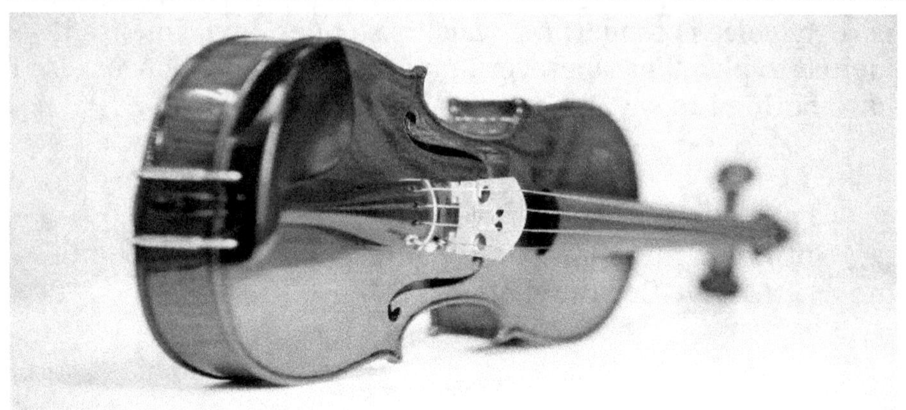

126) Violin

127) Time

128) Eight

129) Coat of paint

130) News

Questions 27

131) What starts with a t, ends with a t, and has t in it?

132) What tastes better than it smells?

133) What is harder to catch the faster you run?

134) How far can you walk into the woods?

135) I am four times my daughter's age. In 20 years, I will be twice her age. How old are we now?

Answers 27

131) Teapot

132) Your tongue

133) Your breath

134) Halfway — After that, you're walking out.

135) I am 40, and my daughter is 10.

Questions 28

136) What do you throw out when you want to use it but take in when you don't want to use it?

137) Put a coin into an empty bottle and insert a cork into the neck. How can you remove the coin without removing the cork or breaking the bottle?

138) How can a man who shaves several times a day still sport a long beard?

139) I come from a mine and am surrounded by wood. I help others to express themselves. What am I?

140) How is seven different from the rest of the numbers between one and ten?

Answers 28

136) Anchor

137) Push the cork down into the bottle; then shake the coin out.

138) He's a barber.

139) Pencil lead

140) It has two syllables.

Questions 29

141) Before Mount Everest was discovered, what was the highest mountain on the earth?

142) How can you physically stand behind your father while he is standing behind you?

143) Two people were playing chess, and both won. How did this happen?

144) Here's a list of sports: golf, darts, tennis, cricket, football, badminton. Which should come next: archery, boxing, squash, gymnastics, or baseball?

145) I can fly, but I have no wings. I can cry, but I have no eyes. Wherever I go, darkness follows me. What am I?

Answers 29

141) Mount Everest

142) You are standing back-to-back with your father.

143) They were playing against other opponents.

144) Gymnastics - Each sport has one more letter than the sport before: badminton has nine, so gymnastics has 10.

145) Cloud

Questions 30

146) What has thirteen hearts but no other organs?

147) Bill is put in a cell with a dirt floor and only one window. The window is too high for him to reach, and the only thing in the cell is a shovel. He won't be able to get any food or water and only has two days to escape or he'll die. Bill can't dig a tunnel because it will take him much longer than two days. How will Bill escape from the cell?

148) You walk into a room and see a bed. On the bed, there are two dogs, five cats, a giraffe, six cows, and a goose. There are also three doves flying above the bed. How many legs are on the floor?

149) A farmer owns a beautiful pear tree and supplies the fruit to a nearby grocery store. The store owner calls the farmer to see how much fruit is available to buy. The farmer knows the main trunk has 24 branches. Each branch has exactly 12 boughs, and each bough has exactly 6 twigs. Since each twig bears one piece of fruit, how many plums will the farmer be able to deliver?

150) I am a five-letter word, and people eat me. If you remove the first letter, I become an energy form. If you remove the first two letters, I am needed to live. Scramble the last three letters, and I am a drink. What word am I?

Answers 30

146) Deck of cards

147) Bill uses the shovel to create a pile of dirt under the window, so he can climb up onto it and escape.

148) Six - the bed's four legs, plus your two legs.

149) None - A pear tree doesn't grow plums.

150) Wheat

Questions 31

151) They have not flesh, nor feathers, nor scales, nor bone, yet they have fingers and thumbs of their own. What are they?

152) A prisoner is called to be questioned by the guards. The guards tell the prisoner, "If you tell a lie, we will hang you, and if you tell the truth, we will shoot you." What did the prisoner say to save himself?

153) How can you throw a ball as hard as you can only to have it come back to you without it bouncing off anything?

154) Steve was murdered on Saturday afternoon. His wife said she was reading; the doorman said he was in the shower. The chef said he was making breakfast. The gardener was pruning hedges. From the information given, who committed the murder?

155) Two girls were born to the same mother, on the same day, at the same time, in the same month, and in the same year, however, they're not twins. How is this possible?

Answers 31

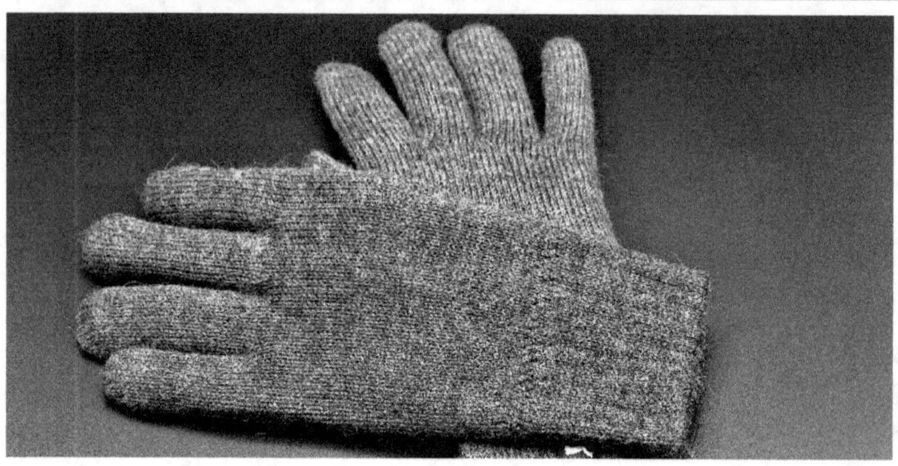

151) Gloves

152) You will hang me.

153) Throw it straight up.

154) Chef – Steve was murdered in the afternoon, yet the chef's alibi was that he was making breakfast.

155) The two girls are a part of a set of triplets.

Questions 32

156) What is full of holes but still holds water?

157) Which English word is the odd one out: stun, ton, evil, letter, mood, bad, strap, snap, and straw?

158) My buddies and I were inseparable mates until one by one we were split. My teacher then gave me a smack on the head, so off in the corner I sit. What am I?

159) A man runs away from home, turns left three times, and ends up back at home facing a man in a mask. Who is wearing the mask?

160) What is it that no one wants, but no one wants to lose?

Answers 32

156) Sponge

157) Letter – It is the only one that does not spell another word when it's written backward.

158) Staple

159) Catcher – It is a baseball game.

160) Lawsuit

Questions 33

161) If a rooster laid a brown egg and a white egg, what kind of chicks would hatch?

162) We hurt without moving and poison without touching. We bear truth and lies but are not judged by size. What are we?

163) A girl has an equal number of brothers and sisters, but each brother only has half as many brothers as sisters. What's the correct number of brothers and sisters?

164) The combined age of a father and son is 66 years, and the age of the father is the age of the son with reversed digits. How old are they?

165) I am a three-digit number. My second digit is four times bigger than the third digit. My first digit is three less than my second digit. Who am I?

Answers 33

161) Roosters don't lay eggs.

162) Words

163) Four sisters and three brothers

164) There are three possible answers – 15 and 51, 42 and 24, or 60 and 06.

165) 141

Questions 34

166) Two camels were facing in opposite directions; one was facing due east, and one was facing due west. They were in the desert, so there was no reflection. How can they manage to see each other without walking around, turning around, or moving their heads?

167) There are three boxes labeled apples, oranges, and apples & oranges. You know that each is labeled incorrectly. You may pick one fruit from one box to determine how they should be labeled; which box should you choose from?

168) You are trapped in a room with two doors. One leads to certain death, and the other leads to freedom. You don't know which is which. There is a guard at each door; they will let you choose one door, but then you must go through it. You can ask one guard one question. The problem is one guard always tells the truth, and the other always lies, and you don't know which is which. What question should you ask?

169) You can paddle your canoe at 7 mph on a placid lake. A stream flows at 3 mph, and the moment you start to paddle upstream, a fisherman loses one of his bobbers in the water 14 miles upstream of you. How long does it take for you and the bobber to meet?

170) Cathy has twelve black socks and twelve white socks in her drawer. In complete darkness, and without looking, how many socks must she take from the drawer to be sure to get a pair that match?

Answers 34

166) The two camels were facing each other; thus, they were facing in opposite directions.

167) Pick from the one labeled apples & oranges; it must contain either only apples or only oranges.

168) Ask one guard what the other guard would say if they were asked which door was safe. Then, go through the other door.

169) Two hours – You are traveling at 4 mph upstream (7 mph – 3 mph for going against the current), and the bobber is traveling at 3 mph, for a combined speed of 7 mph, which covers the 14 miles in 2 hours.

170) Three – With three, you will have to have at least two of one color.

Questions 35

171) I have cities, but not houses. I have mountains, but no trees. I have coasts, but no sand. What am I?

172) Spelled out in English, what is the second number alphabetically no matter how high you go?

173) The day before yesterday I was 21, and next year, I will be 24. When is my birthday?

174) I am a word that begins with the letter "i." If you add the letter "a" to me, I become a new word with a different meaning, but that sounds the same. What word am I?

175) What can fill a room but takes up no space?

Answers 35

171) Map

172) Eight billion

173) December 31; today is January 1.

174) Isle - add "a" to make aisle

175) Light

Questions 36

176) No matter how little or how much you use me, you change me every month. What am I?

177) I turn once; what is out will not get in. I turn again; what is in will not get out. What am I?

178) People make me, save me, change me, raise me. What am I?

179) I go around in circles but always straight ahead. I never complain no matter where I am led. What am I?

180) You have me today; tomorrow you'll have more. As your time passes, I'm not easy to store. I don't take up space, but I'm only in one place. I am what you saw, but not what you see. What am I?

Answers 36

176) Calendar

177) Key

178) Money

179) Wheel

180) Memories

Questions 37

181) A sundial has the fewest moving parts of any timepiece. Which has the most?

182) Twelve apples are hanging on a tree, and twelve men pass by. Each took an apple, and there were eleven apples still on the tree. How can this be?

183) What goes on four legs in the morning, on two legs at noon, and on three legs in the evening?

184) What is red and smells like paint?

185) What is always hungry but never thirsty?

Answers 37

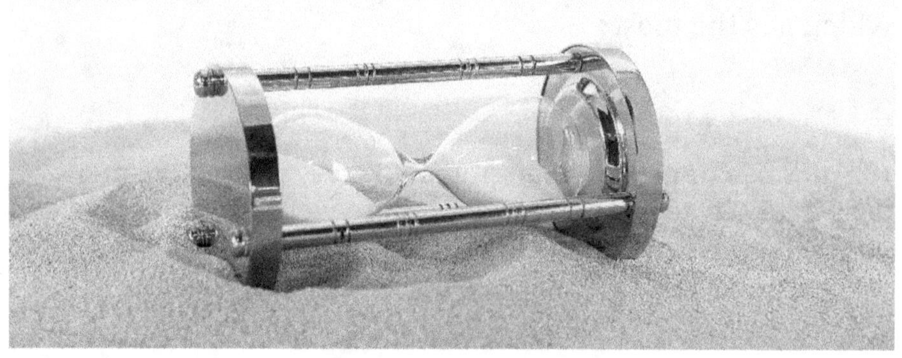

181) An hourglass—It has thousands of grains of sand.

182) "Each" is the name of a person.

183) This is the famous Riddle of the Sphinx describing man. First, as a baby crawling on all fours, then walking on two feet, and as an elderly person with a walking stick.

184) Red paint

185) Fire

Questions 38

186) What jumps when walking and sits when standing?

187) It is an insect, and the first part of its name is the name of another insect. What is it?

188) What is as big as an elephant but weighs nothing at all?

189) One knight, a ninja, and a pirate are on a boat, and the boat crashes. The pirate jumps off first; the ninja jumps off second; who jumps off third?

190) If there are three cups of sugar, and you take one away, how many do you have?

Answers 38

186) Kangaroo

187) Beetle

188) The shadow of an elephant

189) The knight – People think the opening reads, "One night," not "One knight."

190) One cup - That is what you took away.

Questions 39

191) I possess a halo of water, walls of stone, and a tongue of wood. Long I have stood; what am I?

192) Each day many people from all over the world come and visit me; however, they usually only stay for a couple of minutes. I am considered by many to be very dirty; yet few people would want to live without me, and whenever people come to see me, they show a part of themselves that they rarely show to others. What am I?

193) John pointed to a girl in the street and said, "She is the daughter of my grandmother's only child." What is the girl's relationship to John?

194) Four people arrive at a river with a narrow bridge that can only hold two people at a time. It's nighttime, and they have one torch that must be used when crossing the bridge. Person A can cross the bridge in one minute, B in two minutes, C in five minutes, and D in eight minutes. When two people cross the bridge together, they must move at the slower person's pace. Can they all get across the bridge in 15 minutes or less?

195) When Billy is asked how old he is, he answers, "In two years, I will be twice as old as I used to be five years ago." How old is he?

Answers 39

191) Castle

192) Toilet

193) She is his sister.

194) Yes, they can cross in exactly 15 minutes. First, A and B cross the bridge, and A brings the light back. This takes 3 minutes. Next, C and D cross, and B brings the light back. This takes another 10 minutes. Finally, A and B cross again. This takes another 2 minutes.

195) 12 years old

Questions 40

196) This vehicle is spelled the same forward and backward. What is it?

197) The brother of Nick's uncle Manny is named Mark. Lisa's grandparents are Nick's parents. Mark is married to Lisa's grandma. The children of Angela's daughter Sandra are named Lisa and Sasha. Who is Angela's brother-in-law?

198) There is a house; one enters it blind and comes out seeing. What is it?

199) Spelled out in English, what is the only number whose letters are in reverse alphabetical order?

200) A train is leaving Chicago and heading for New York at 60 mph. Three hours later, a train leaves New York heading for Chicago at 80 mph. Assume there are 700 miles between Chicago and New York. When the trains meet, which train is closest to Chicago?

Answers 40

196) Racecar – spelled the same forward and backward

197) Manny is Angela's brother-in-law.

198) School – This is one of the oldest known written riddles from ancient Sumer, current day Iraq.

199) One

200) When they meet, the trains are in the same location and the same distance from Chicago.

Bonus Riddle

This logic puzzle is often attributed to Albert Einstein. The story is that Einstein wrote it when he was a young man, and he estimated that only two percent of the people who tried to solve it would be successful.

There are five houses; each is painted a different color. In each house lives a person of a different nationality. Each owner drinks a certain type of beverage, smokes a certain brand of cigar, and keeps a certain pet. No two owners have the same pet, smoke the same cigar, or drink the same beverage.

- The Brit lives in the red house
- The Swede keeps dogs as pets
- The Dane drinks tea
- The green house is on the left of the white house
- The green house's owner drinks coffee
- The person who smokes Pall Mall rears birds
- The owner of the yellow house smokes Dunhill
- The man living in the center house drinks milk
- The Norwegian lives in the first house
- The man who smokes blends lives next to the one who keeps cats
- The man who keeps horses lives next to the man who smokes Dunhill
- The owner who smokes BlueMaster drinks beer
- The German smokes Prince
- The Norwegian lives next to the blue house
- The man who smokes blend has a neighbor who drinks water

Based on this information, who owns the fish?

Bonus Riddle Answer

The German owns the fish.

German – green house, fish, coffee, Prince
Norwegian – yellow house, cats, water, Dunhill
Dane– blue house, horse, tea, Blends
Brit – red house, birds, milk, Pall Mall
Swede – white house, dogs, beer, Bluemaster

If you enjoyed this book and would like others to enjoy it also, please put out a review or rating.